UNIFORMS ILLUSTRATED NO. 13

UNIFORMS ILLUSTRATED NO. 13

BRITISH SPECIAL FORCES
1945 to the present

JAMES G. SHORTT

a&ap
ARMS AND ARMOUR PRESS

Introduction

Published in 1986 by Arms & Armour Press Ltd., 2–6 Hampstead High Street, London NW3 1QQ.

Distributed in the United States by Sterling Publishing Co. Inc., 2 Park Avenue, New York, N.Y. 10016.

British Library Cataloguing in Publication Data:
Shortt, James G.
British special forces : 1945 to the present.
—(Uniforms illustrated; v. 13)
1. Great Britain. *Army. Special Forces* —
Uniforms—History
I. Title II. Series
355.1′4′0941 UC485.G7

ISBN 0–85368–785–4

Editing, design and artwork by Roger Chesneau.
Typesetting by Typesetters (Birmingham) Ltd.
Printed and bound in Italy
by GEA/GEP in association with
Keats European Ltd., London.

◀**1**

1. Members of 22 SAS listen intently at a pre-exercise briefing in April 1968. The exercise in Brightstone Forest on the Isle of Wight was called 'Sabotage' and placed the SAS in an anti-terrorist/anti-Spestnaz role working with the British police in what was to be the start of a long liaison in these matters. (22 SAS)

In every age of war there have been the élite. They are the élite because they train harder and more realistically than their contemporaries in conventional forces; because, for their numbers, they accomplish more than their contemporaries; and because, to survive as a unit, they invariably have to wage another kind of war against leaders within their own army – leaders jealous of their accomplishments and jealous of the honours bestowed upon them. In the past these élite troops would have been constantly before the public gaze as an example of service to the nation, but in our own times they are obliged not to disclose their identities in order to protect their roles, their future missions and even their lives and those of their families.

The photographs in this book have been provided by the units and members of the units that make up the British Special Forces. Where an illustration has been donated by a Special Forces veteran, the credit has been given to his unit. In many of the photographs, in the interests of security and in certain cases the personal safety of a serviceman, facial features have been deliberately obscured in order to prevent recognition. I do not feel that this in any way detracts from the value of this book as a unique catalogue of achievement.

By 1945, the starting point for this book, existing British Special Forces had inherited a wartime tradition from such units as the Special Air Service (SAS), Raiding Forces, Special Boat Squadron (SBS), Special Reconnaissance Squadron (SRS), Long Range Desert Group (LRDG) and Special Operations Executive (SOE) to name but a few. A postwar rationalization reduced British Special Forces to a Small Raid Wing within the Royal Marines who had taken on board the Commando/raiding role and one Special Air Service regiment, the 21st, a territorial army unit raised under the badge of the Artist Rifles. Since then, as this book will relate, British Special Forces have grown, and units operating in support of conventional forces have included a regular (22nd) and another TA (23rd) SAS Regiment; six Special Boat Sections raised under a Special Boat Squadron, Royal Marines; and Royal Naval Clearance Divers working in underwater demolition and beach reconnaissance roles. To these must be added the Royal Navy Submarine Parachute Assistance Groups (SPAG), the parachute-trained Ammunition Technicians of the RAOC and the Special Reconnaissance Squadron of the Royal Armoured Corps, whilst during the Borneo Campaign the SAS recruited the Gurkha Parachute Company, the Guards Parachute Company and 'C' Company of the 2nd Battalion the Parachute Regiment for the SAS role. The Paras were of course no strangers to these tasks, having provided a Para Squadron for the 22nd SAS during the Malaya Campaign. There are other smaller units that have operated in a specialist role in the past forty years. They do not appear here and cannot be mentioned at present. Perhaps in the future . . . ?

My thanks to the Special Forces.

James G. Shortt

▲2

3 

◀4

2. A postwar photograph of members of the School of Combined Operations Beach & Boat Section (SCOBBS) then based at Fremington, North Devon. This group is composed for the most part of Royal Marines. The RM officer is wearing the distinctive dark battle-dress, and several men have Parachute qualification wings, at least one wearing them in the old operational style on the left breast. Four members of the Royal Navy are also included in this section. When the Royal Marines took over the swimmer-canoeist role exclusively in 1946 all personnel were moved to RM Eastney, near Portsmouth, where they evolved into the Small Raids Wing in October 1947. (SBS)

3. Early 1949: men of 'A' Squadron, 21st Special Air Service (Artists) Volunteers, emplane in a Dakota under the watchful gaze of their CO, Lt. Col. Ian Lapraik. Col. Lapraik had served in the SAS's Special Boat Squadron in the Mediterranean during the war, and on the creation of 21 SAS he recruited many wartime SAS and SBS veterans into its ranks, whilst within 'B' Squadron 21 SAS he formed an amphibious arm. The distinctive 21st Special Air Service Artists shoulder titles are worn on the colonel's BD jacket; all personnel wear 'Artist Rifles' cap badges on maroon berets, and many wear the camouflaged SAS windproofs introduced during the Second World War. (21 SAS)

4. Royal Naval Clearance Divers are pulled from the water at high speed during Exercise 'Run Aground' off the coast at Southsea in July 1950. These frogmen worked alongside the Small Raids Wing and Landing Craft Wing of the Royal Marines at nearby RM Eastney, engaging in beach reconnaissance and clearance with the swimmer-canoeists in advance of Royal Marine landings. (SBS)

▲5 ▼6

5. Malaya 1951–53: a very rare group photograph of 'C' Squadron 22 SAS, formed from Rhodesian Commonwealth personnel and led by their CO, Major Walls, who later became Commander of Rhodesian Combined Operations after UDI. Lt. Col. Sloane, CO 22 SAS (centre, seated), wears distinctive SAS 'pea greens' whilst the remainder of the squadron wear No. 6 dress and the airborne maroon beret with cloth SAS badge. (SAS Association)
6. A 22 SAS officer in Malaya wearing the 'X' type parachute developed by the GQ company. Over his No. 7 dress, which displays SAS 'Sabre' wings, he wears a Second World War Airborne smock, and he has tucked his maroon beret (with SAS badge) into the 'chute straps. Having parachuted in to the 200ft high jungle canopy he will climb down this rope to reach the jungle floor. (SAS Association)
7. 22 SAS mounts a guard of honour for an RAF officer in Malaya, 1956. The men are kitted out in No. 6 dress, with the Malaya command patch on either sleeve. Parachute wings are visible on the SAS officer's right shoulder. (22 SAS)
8. The RSM of 22 SAS wearing 'pea greens' privately tailored in Penang for regimental officers and senior warrant officers. Around him are NCOs of the regiment wearing white No. 3 parade dress with SAS 'collar dogs'.

23

7▲ 8▼

▲9 ▼10

11▲

9. The Royal Marine Special Boat Wing, responsible for training swimmer-canoeists for Nos. 1 and 2 Special Boat Sections, poses beneath the unit's unofficial emblem, a winged frog seated on crossed canoe paddles, August 1950. In the foreground is an early one-man experimental canoe. Note the presence of naval personnel to teach boatcraft and seamanship within the wing; notice also that parachute qualification wings are not being worn. This photograph was taken at the Wing HQ at RM Eastney. (SBS)

10. A Royal Marine Physical Training Instructor teaches SBS swimmer-canoeists unarmed combat based on the original Fairbairn Commando method. The PTI is wearing a Denison smock and lightweight cotton trousers, by then standard combat dress for the Royal Marines and the Parachute Regiment. Instead of the 1944-pattern web belt he has cord to hold the smock in place, and he is wearing regulation PT shoes. (SBS)

11. A group photograph of Royal Marine swinner-canoeists in 'diving rig'. They wear dry suits, fins and closed-circuit oxygen re-breather sets, with the mask visible held at the left shoulder. (SBS)

12. Members of 6 SBS, formed in Malta in 1957 to act in direct support of 3 Commando Brigade, who were stationed on the island at the time. 6 SBS later moved to the Far East, returning to the United Kingdom in 1971. The men are wearing hot weather dress, with the Royal Marine stable belt in evidence. (6 SBS)

12▼

▲13

13. Members of the Special Boat Company (formerly the Special Boat Unit, Special Boat Wing and Small Raids Wing) put on a demonstration of skills in the 168ft × 48ft static tank at their base at RM Eastney, 22 July 1959. Visible are a paddle board, a Gemini inflatable Mk. 1* and an Army engineer assault inflatable boat. The Gemini is powered by a Johnson engine. (SBS)

14. Royal Marine swimmer-canoeists, wearing a mixture of windproof smocks and at least one Denison smock, show off their new Mk. 1* canoes prior to the London Boat Show in December 1959. Note the external inflated buoyancy bladders and the lifting handles featured both by this model and by the Mk. 1**. (SBS)

15. The RM SB Company in the early 1960s, with members of 1, 2 and 3 Special Boat Sections; in the foreground, a Mk. 1* canoe displays their many trophies for sporting prowess. Dress comprises the regulation KD shirts with BD trousers and 1938-pattern webbing belt blackened and polished. (SBS)

14▲ 15▼

▲16

▲17 ▼18

16. Two members of 22 SAS undergo ski-ing instruction by a German Alpine NCO in the Bavarian Alps. The regiment had returned from combat in Malaya and Borneo in 1959 and used the 'quiet' 1960–61 period to develop unit skills. These two SAS troopers wear the 'commando' pullover with neck drawstring and British Army ski cap; their instructor wears the distinctive 'edelweiss' mountain badge on his battle-dress jacket. (22 SAS)

17. A 22 SAS sergeant in a patrol vehicle of one of the Squadron's Land Rover troops (later to become Mobility troops). Note the Browning Mk. 2 .30 at the rear, the side-mounted Bren .303 and the twin Vickers 'K'. This NCO wears an Airborne Denison smock. (22 SAS)

18. Wearing distinctive wind-proof smocks and SAS berets, Land Rover troop members bring their Browning to bear during trials of the new vehicles in the mid-1960s. Note that the vehicle has been stripped of windscreen and doors and that the spare tyre has been arranged so as to protect the radiator grille. (22 SAS)

19, 20. Borneo 1963: members of the Guards Independent Parachute Company (part of the 16th Parachute Brigade) are taken into an SAS role by 22 SAS, along with the Gurkha Parachute Company and 'C' (Patrol) Company of 2 Para. At this time 22 SAS consisted of 'A' & 'D' Squadrons and an HQ and was somewhat thin on the ground. The Borneo campaign lasted from 1962 until 1966 and was overlapped by the Aden campaign of 1964–67, which meant that at the height of the operations the squadrons rotated. As a result, it was suggested that SAS squadrons be created by forming nine units, drawing three each from the Guards, Gurkhas and Paras, but the proposal was turned down. Here Guards Para members try their newly issued Armalite 5.56mms for the first time. Note the Parachute Regiment beret badge, parachute wings and SAS-style belt kits in place of the 1958-pattern CEFO; note also that slings and sling pivots have been removed from the weapons. (GIPC)

19▲ 20▼

▲21

21. Members of the Guards Company unload their vehicles and equipment from a Royal Marine Commando landing craft (LCVP) under the gaze of members of 22 SAS, Borneo, 1964.

22. A Whirlwind helicopter brings members of the Guards Company to their jungle base in Borneo. (GIPC)

23, 24. An RAF Whirlwind helicopter is refuelled at the Guards Company base prior to the deployment of a four-man patrol. Lack of electricity means that refuelling is done with the aid of a portable diesel generator. Members of the patrol can be seen in their jungle greens about to mount the helicopter prior to insertion; support personnel drawn from the Army and the RAF are also in attendance. (GIPC)

▼22

23▲ 24▼

▲25 ▼26

25. On longe-range patrol: a member of the Guards Company ports his SLR in a cradle, wary of a contact with Indonesian irregulars. Note the cut-down bush hat and the cord from it to the shirt. (GIPC)
26. A Para Guardsman sets an explosive charge amongst the roots of a fallen tree that bridges a fast-flowing Borneo river. The beard and hair are long by British Army standards of the day. (GIPC)
27. A Guards soldier with his Armalite sits on a woodpile in an Iban village, 1965. The jungle living has taken its toll in weight reduction through loss of body fluid. (GIPC)
28. Members of the Guards Independent Parachute Company await a flight back to Britain from Singapore in 1966, having fought a very successful war in the SAS role. (GIPC)

27▲ 28▼

▲29 ▼30

31▲

◀32

29. Back at the Guards Depot at Pirbright, the Parachute Company returns to its normal role in support of the 16th Parachute Brigade. When the brigade was disbanded in 1975, so too was the Guards Company. (GIPC)

30. Members of 22 SAS pose with their troop officer, Borneo, 1965. They wear No. 7 warm weather working dress, 1944-pattern belts and boots DMS with puttees; all have 'Sabre' SAS wings, and the cyphers 'SAS' appear on the officer's rank slides. (22 SAS)

31. Members of 'G' Squadron's mobility troop photographed on exercise with camouflaged Long-Range Land Rovers and armed with Brownings. (22 SAS)

32. Members of 22 SAS relax outside 'The House', their base within the 'Little Aden' barracks that were their home during the 1964–67 war. Parked in front are the long-wheelbase Land Rovers that were later to be nicknamed 'Pink Panthers' (22 SAS)

▲33 ▼34 35▶

33. A 'Green Beret' sergeant of the US 10th Special Forces Group talks to visiting members of 22 SAS at the 10th's German home at Bad Tolz, where many of the SAS who had not trained in the USA earned US Parachute wings. The US sergeant wears the Special Forces badge on a green shield; the SAS soldier nearest the camera wears a windproof camouflage smock and the SAS beige beret. The photograph was taken in 1968. (22 SAS)
34. A member of 22 SAS parachuting at Fort Bragg, North Carolina, Headquarters of the US Special Forces. (22 SAS)
35. Members of the Royal Armoured Corps' Special Reconnaissance Squadron (SRS) practise unarmed combat at their base in West Germany with the BAOR. The SRS was formed in May 1962 to act in a target designation and long-range reconnaissance role for the RAC. It was selected and trained at Hereford by the SAS. (RAC)

▲36 ▼37 38▶

36, 37. The SRS operated from May 1962 until February 1965. In August 1962 'C' Squadron of the 2nd Royal Tank Regiment was trained in an airborne short-range reconnaissance role for the RAC as 'Cyclops'. This photograph, taken in Germany, shows joint training for SRS and Cyclops members in the use of the Sterling SMG and grenade throwing. Note the Denison smocks and the SAS beret with parent regiment badge.
38. A member of the élite Royal Marines Mountain and Arctic Warfare Cadre, Britain's only mountain troops (apart from the SAS squadrons' various climbing troops), stands in a snow cave entrance wearing white winter camouflage.

▲39 ▼40

39. An M&AWC patrol moves in file along the slopes of a Scottish mountainside during an exercise. The men carry climbing ropes and Armalite rifles and wear the arctic smock designed for the Royal Marines' winter warfare role.
40. A Cadre member hauls his load-carrying equipment up a snow slope to the summit of a Scottish mountain. The major role of the Cadre is long-range reconnaissance for 3 Commando Brigade operating in Norway – a role it must carry out regardless of weather conditions.
41. An NCO of the Cadre stands to with his patrol, having exited from woodland where the men have spent the night. The Cadre served with distinction in the Falklands, recording a resounding victory against Argentine Special Forces who had been parachuted behind British patrol lines at Top Malo House.
42. Cornwall is the site chosen by the Mountain and Arctic Warfare Cadre for developing rock-climbing skills. New recruits are taught basic ascent, descent and belaying skills on the cliffs around the duchy's coast.

41▲ 42▼

▲43 ▼44

43. Black canopies in the snow of a Norwegian valley demonstrate the Cadre's parachute capability. Apart from the SBS, the Cadre is the only Royal Marine unit that requires parachute skills for service in its ranks.

44. Two SBS divers measure the gradient of a beach and take samples in a reconnaissance exercise. The SBS carried out this type of operation prior to the San Carlos landings in the Falklands War.

45. In February 1962 both Cyclops and SRS were disbanded and cadres from each unit merged at Tidworth to become the Parachute Squadron of the Royal Armoured Corps under the former CO of the SRS, Maj. G. K. Bidie. The Squadron operated as long-range anti-tank defence for the 16th Parachute Brigade. The two paras in the photograph wear Denison smocks and the maroon beret with RAC badge. (RAC)

46. 'Prisoners' are searched and questioned by SAS NCOs (who wear no rank indications) prior to being taken for interrogation by the Intelligence Corps during a training exercise. (22 SAS)

45▲ 46▼

A
SPECIAL AIR SERVICE
B
C
D
E
S.A.S. REGIMENT
MALAYAN SCOUTS
THE MALAYAN SCOUTS
S A S
F
S.A.S.
G
H
SPECIAL AIR SERVICE
(ARTISTS)
I
J
ARTISTS
K
L

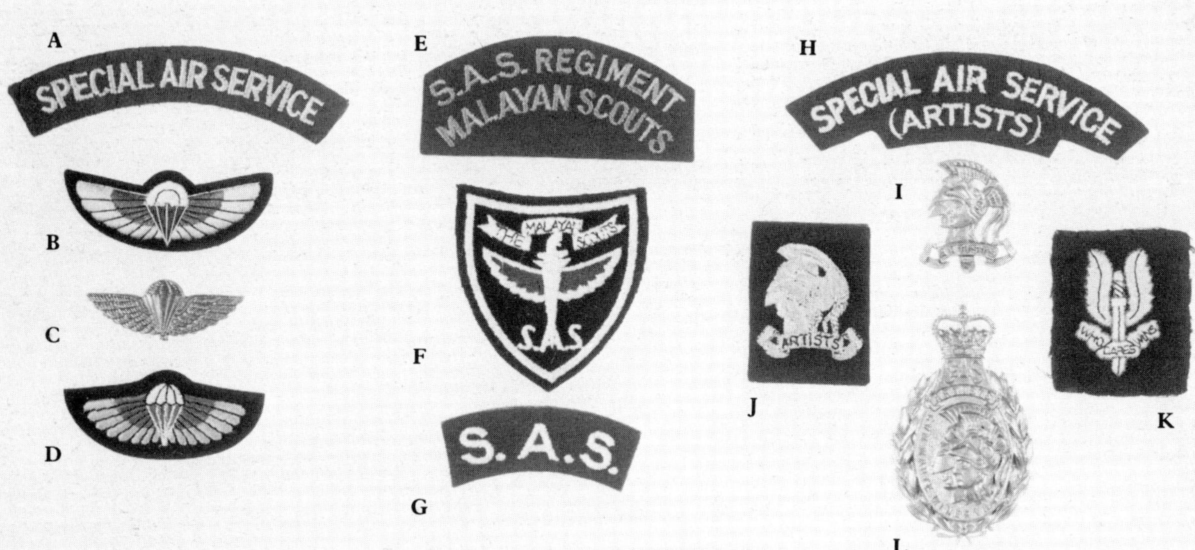

▲48 ▼49

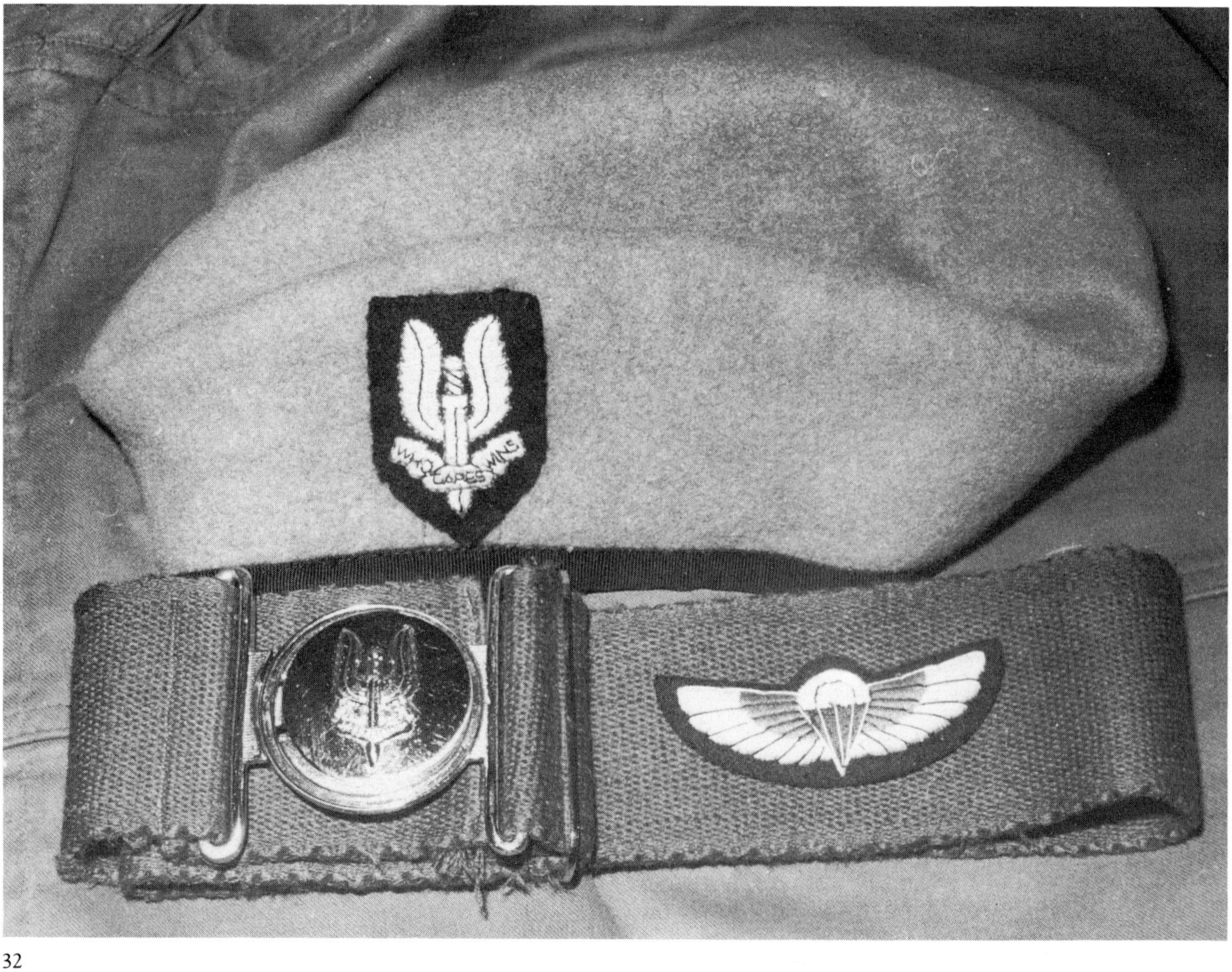

50▲

51▲ 52▼

47. (Previous spread) Members of 22 SAS round up would-be saboteurs drawn for exercise purposes from their own ranks and from 16 Para Brigade. The SAS men search clothing and equipment whilst prisoners wearing Denison and windproof smocks are made to remove their boots and loosen their clothing. (22 SAS)
48. British Special Forces insignia: **A.** 22 SAS shoulder title; **B.** 21 and 22 SAS wings; **C.** Tropical wings; **D.** 23 SAS wings; **E.** Malayan Scouts shoulder title; **F.** Malayan Scouts arm shield; **G.** 21/22/23 SAS title; **H.** 21 SAS shoulder title; **I.** 21 SAS beret badge; **J.** 2nd Ptn. 21 SAS arm badge; **K.** 1st Ptn. 21 SAS arm badge; **L.** 21 SAS cross belt badge. (Author's Collection)
49. Beige beret and cloth SAS shield, SAS stable belt (blue with silver) and parachute qualification wings. (Author's Collection)
50. Officer's bullion beret badge, SAS. (Author's Collection)
51. NCOs' and ORs' rank slides of the SAS: Trooper, Lance-Corporal, Corporal, Sergeant and Staff Sergeant. (Author's Collection)
52. A unique Parachute qualification badge awarded by 21 SAS to a member of a Base Signals Section attached to them from the women's FANY (First Aid Nursing Yeomanry) in 1961. The FANYs provided signals and agents for the clandestine Special Operation Executive (SOE), Special Forces HQ, during the Second World War. This badge is in the shape of the SAS beret badge with light blue wings, after the design of the 'winged dagger' wings overlaid by a white parachute. (Author)

▲53 ▼54 ▼55

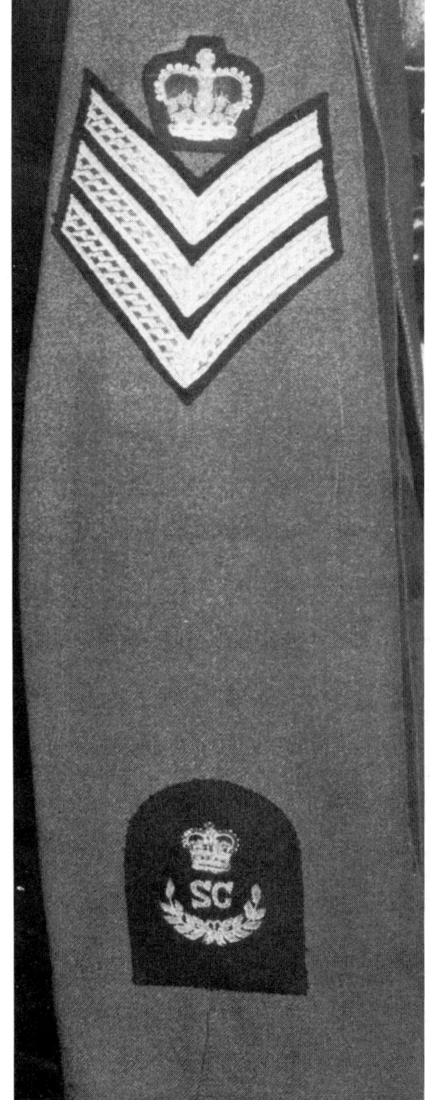

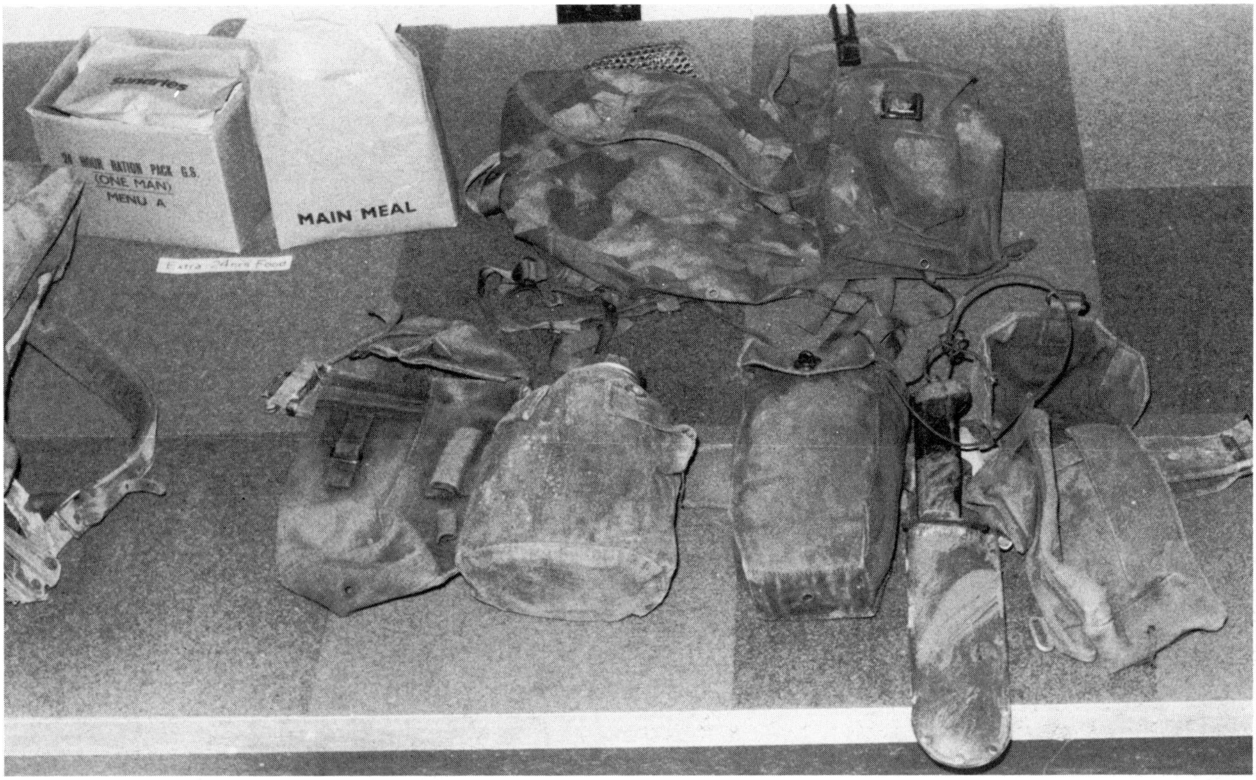

56▲

53. SBS qualification or special quality badges of the Royal Marines in the Royal Navy 'tombstone' format, showing swimmer-canoeist (SC) awards 1, 2 and 3.
54, 55. SBS SC badge as worn on the Lovat dress.
56. The SBS belt kit, comprising a 1958-pattern belt with pouches and MoD survival knife, as displayed in the SBS Ops Room. (Author's Collection)
57. SAS belt kit as issued, showing compass, twin SLR pouches twin 1944-pattern water bottles, rations and altimeter pouches. (Author)

57▼

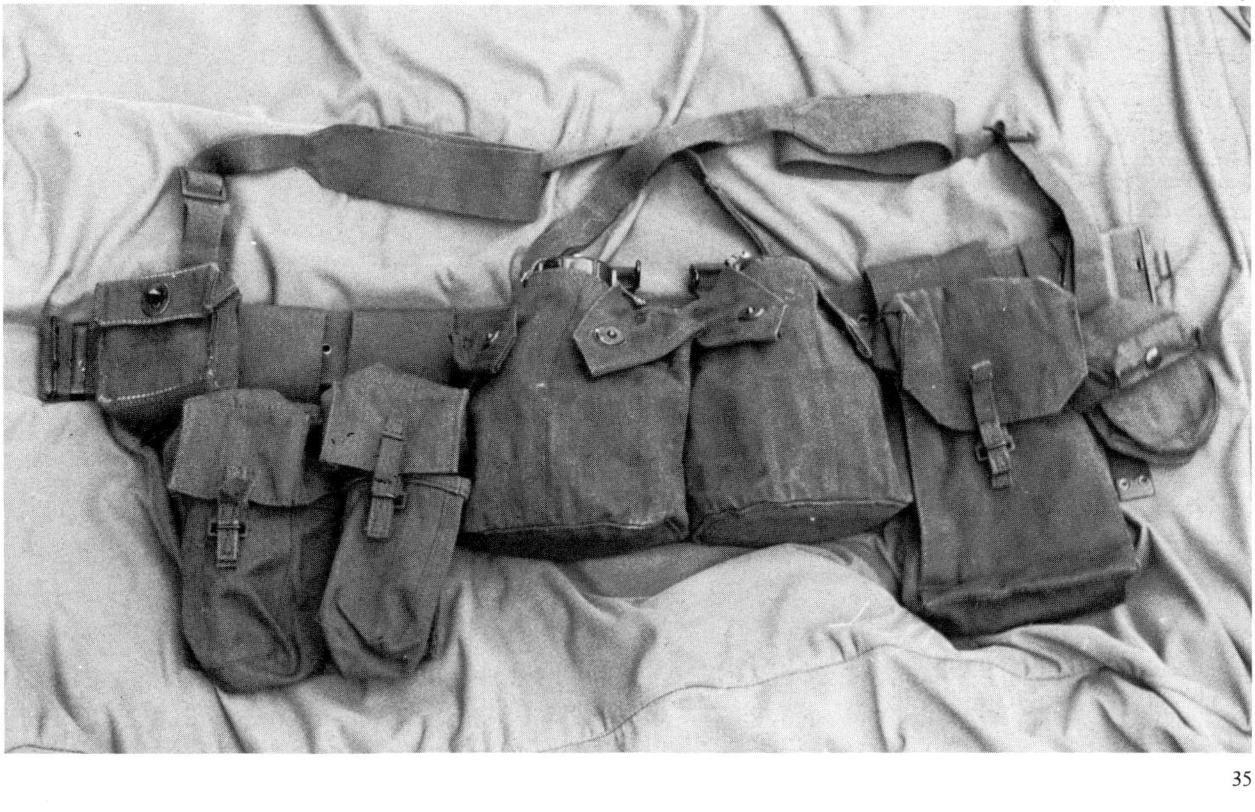

▲58

▲59 ▼60

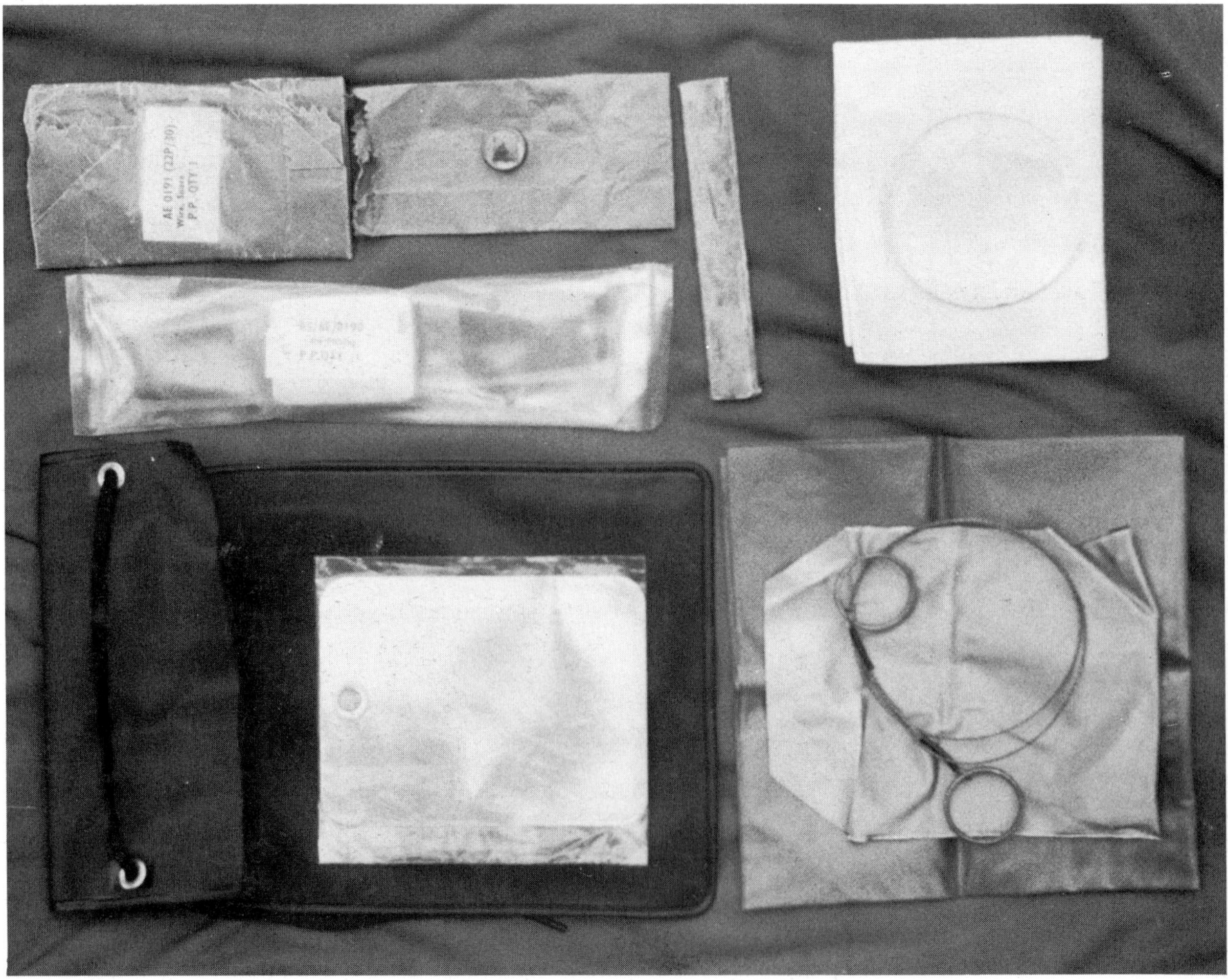

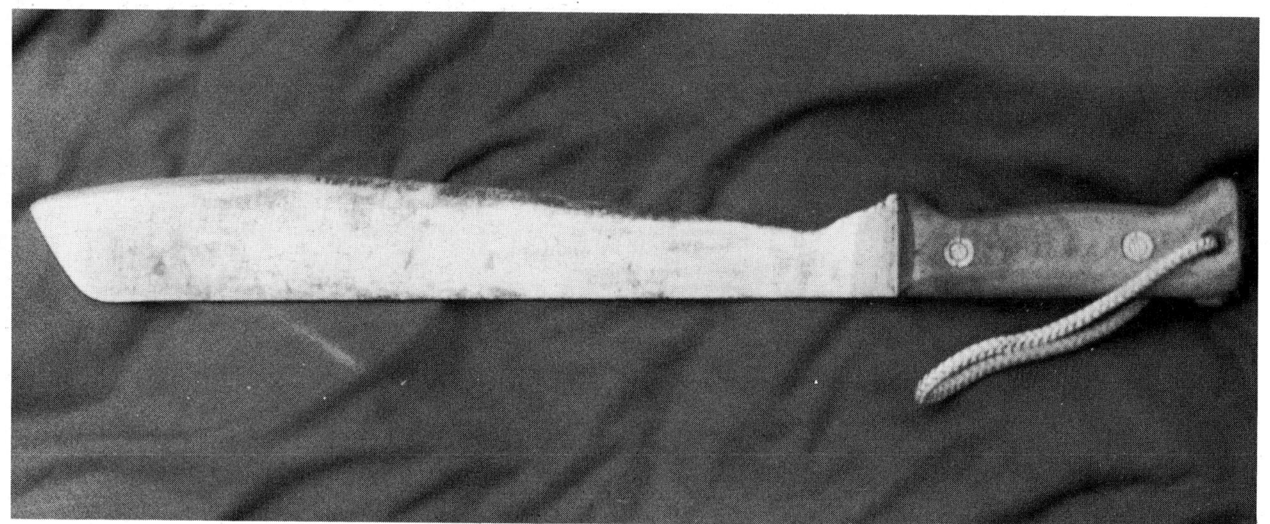

61▲

58. The Royal Navy Para qualification badge for members of SPAG (Submarine Parachute Assistance Group).
59. The unofficial SPAG 'club' badge.
60. SAS-issue Escape and Evasion kit: heliograph, water sacs, lens, button compass, fishing kit, wire snares, wire saw and hacksaw blades. (Author)

61. The golok, a jungle knife named by the SAS and until recently issued only to them and to the Royal Marine Commandos. The original golok is a fighting machette of Indonesian origin. (Author)
62, 63. The current British Special Forces arctic waistcoat, which is to replace the belt kit. It is shown here against a DPM-clad figure. (Author)

62▼

63▼

64. An SBS diver uses his swimboard with depth-gauge and compass to determine his course as he enters the water during SBS training at Squadron HQ, RM Poole, 1971. He wears a wet suit with a closed circuit re-breathing set. (SBS)
65. An SBS team consisting of two swimmers and two canoeists use Klepper canoes for short-range target penetration during training near Poole. (SBS)
66. Two SBS divers enter the water on the final leg of a training exercise to plant explosives under a railway bridge.
67. Members of 23 SAS (based in Northern England and Scotland) rush an Army Bedford truck that they have halted in an exercise ambush in Germany, May 1970. They wear old-pattern SAS windproof smocks, despite the introduction in the British Forces of DPM (Disruptive Pattern Material). (23 SAS)

64▶

▼65

66▲ 67▼

68. Members of 21 SAS mount a Guard of Honour at the Royal Academy, Piccadilly, for the opening of the Summer Exhibition – a custom inherited from their Artist Rifles forebears. Note the Rifle-pattern black and green rank chevrons, the SAS wings and the SAS collar badge on No. 2 dress. (21 SAS)

69, 70. Another Artist tradition lived up to by members of 21 SAS: mounting guard at the Guild of Glovers Ball in the City of London. Note the officer's dress of blues with cross belt of Artist Rifles design. (21 SAS)

◀68

69▲ 70▼

Centrum
Odense
Middelfart

▲72

71. (Previous spread) Three members of 21 SAS in an exercise role as Warsaw Pact infiltrators and saboteurs are captured and searched by members of the Danish Home Guard (HJV). (21 SAS)

72. Two SAS soldiers, one from 22 SAS the other a PSI (22 SAS) with 21 SAS, meet up during an exercise in 1971. They both wear SAS camouflaged windproof smocks with olive green lightweights. (22 SAS)

73. Two SCs in a Klepper ride out the surf.

74. Two SCs of the SBS ride the surf in their Kestrel inflatable. The Kestrel was made of waterproofed lightweight Egyptian cotton and was worn packed in a valise as a leg load for one parachutist, the other carrying the 9½hp engine. Once in the water the craft was inflated using a lanyard that activated the attached CO_2 gas bottle.

73▲ 74▼

75–78. Four photographs illustrating scenes from Operation 'Nimrod', the assault on the Iranian Embassy, London, by 22 SAS, May 1980 (see also photographs 105–115). Members of the assault team gather on the roof of the embassy in their black coveralls and hoods, and with S6 respirators, awaiting final preparations (75). They play out their descent ropes and attach their 'figure of eight' descenders, known as 'bottle-openers' (76), and then their commanding officer's words launch them into the history books and they abseil down on to a balcony at the rear of the building (77). In photograph 78, a lone SAS trooper attempts to free himself from his fouled abseil equipment while the wooden surround of a barricaded window burns, initiated by the heat of a stun grenade. This man was badly injured, but he went on to play a heroic role in the rescue of the hostages.

▲75 ▼76

77▲ 78▼

79. Two members of the Royal Marines Special Boat Squadron set off for another mission.
80. An SAS officer debriefs a patrol from 23 SAS following an exercise in Denmark in 1971. Note the variety of clothing – both olive green and camouflaged windproof smocks. (23 SAS)
81. An SAS officer speaks to NATO Armed Forces commanders at the close of an exercise. Behind them sit members of 21 and 23 SAS.
◀**79**

80▲ 81▼

▲82 ▼83

82. Members of 21 SAS study a map with their OC prior to setting out on a long-range patrol during an exercise in Norway in 1972. (21 SAS)

83, 84, 85. The SAS were committed to the war in the Djebel of Oman from 1972 until its close in 1975. The most outstanding aspect of the war was the way in which the SAS influenced the 'adoo' (enemy, i.e. members of the PFLAG) trained in Communist China and the USSR. The SAS, through their 'hearts and minds' programme, enticed the Djebeli tribesman fighting for the PFLAG to join the SAS-trained and -led 'Firqua' teams. Members of the Firqua armed with captured Russian and Chinese weapons, grenades and RPG2 and RPG7 grenade launchers are shown here; they wear a variety of Arab and British Army clothing. (SAS)

84▲ 85▼

▲86 ▼87

86, 87, 88. Two SAS instructors demonstrate unarmed combat to Kenyan Para Commando troops during a training team visit to camps on the Kenya-Somali border; the SAS have regularly trained in this region since 1959. Photographs 87 and 88 show the Kenyan troops practising what they have been taught under the eye of their SAS instructors. (SAS)
89. SAS instructors teach African Commonwealth troops weapon handling with the Soviet AK47. The troops being taught are members of the Special Forces of the country concerned.

88▲ 89▼

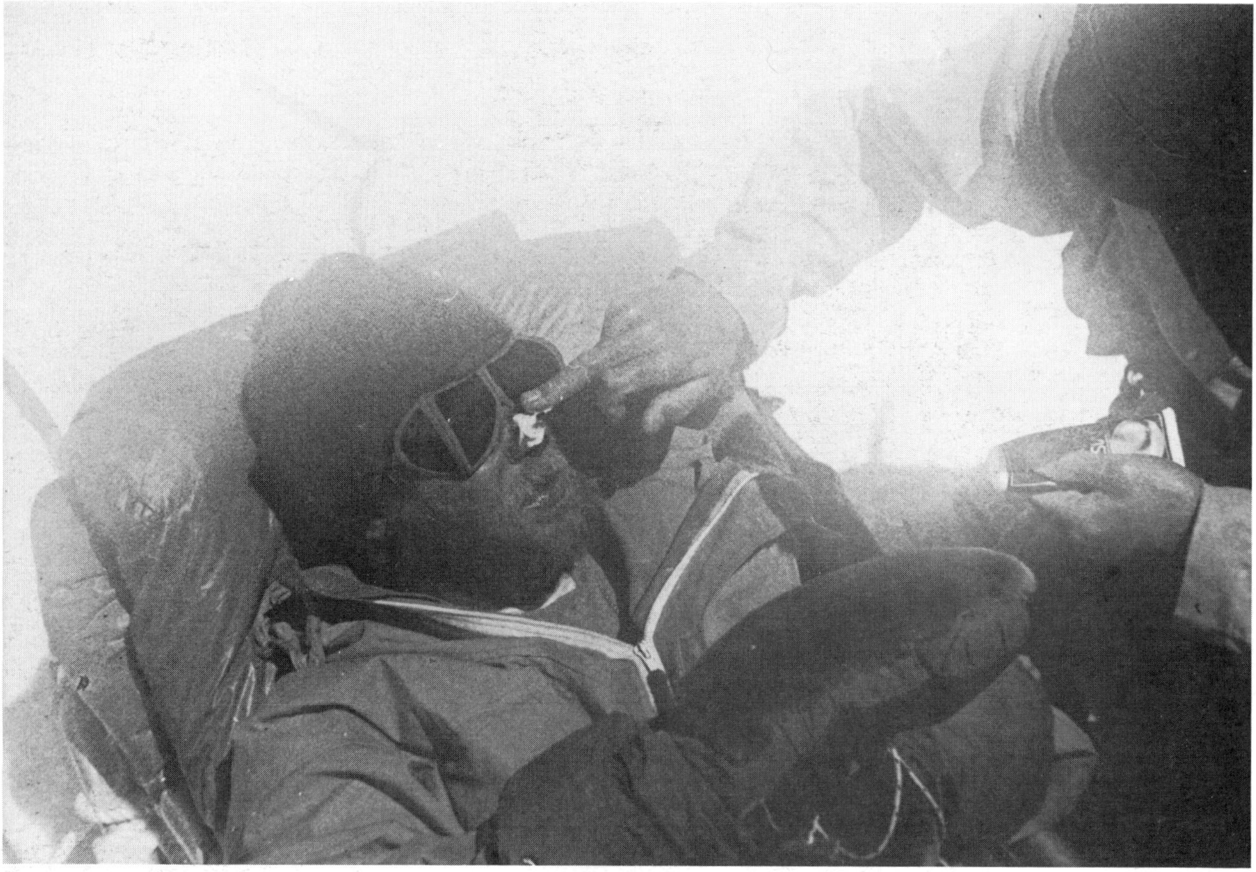

▲90 ▼91

▼92

90. Sgt. John 'Brummie' Stokes and Cpl. Michael 'Bronco' Lane, the first two British soldiers to conquer Everest, May 1976. The expedition, organized by the Army Mountaineering Association in conjunction with the Royal Nepalese Army, cost five lives, and both SAS soldiers lost several toes in the climb. (22 SAS).

91. The EOD (Explosive Ordnance Disposal) officer of the RAOC who jumped with members of the SAS and RM SBS into the Atlantic to search for an IED (improvised explosive device) on board the liner *Queen Elizabeth II* in 1972 was equipped as shown, the valise containing his bomb disposal equipment. Note that, as with most wet jumpers, this parachutist has his swim fins fastened to his lower leg and wears plimsolls and wet suits. (RAOC)

92. Two SAS officers from 21 SAS greet a Danish Army brigadier during joint HJV–SAS exercises in Denmark. Note the bullion beret badge, 'woolly-pully', SAS rank slides and SAS stable belt. (21 SAS)

93. The Parachute EOD role is now in the hands of the Parachute Company of the 11th EOD Battalion RAOC. When a wet jump is required the technician is guided to the target by the RM SBS. Note the wet jump equipment on the table. (RAOC)

93▶

◀94 95▲

94. A TA SAS trooper pictured during an exercise on Barossa Common, Camberley, in 1979; note the use of high-neck boots before the general introduction of this footwear to replace DMS boots and puttees, the SAS windproof smock in DPM pattern and matching combat cap, and the 'personalized' belt kit.
95. Members of 'B' Squadron 21 SAS on patrol during an exercise on Barossa Common in September 1979. Carrying the SAS-pattern butyl laminate square-frame bergen, they move in to practise SAS contact drills. (Author)
96. A 'P' Company fast march for members of 21 and 22 SAS. Hereford, June 1980. (Author)
97. An abseiling harness and horned 'figure of eight' descenders worn over an SAS windproof smock and trousers in DPM. The photograph was taken in June 1980, prior to abseil training on 'The Tower', Hereford, for members of 21 and 23 SAS. (Author)

96▼

97▼

▲98 ▼99

▲100 ▼101

98–101. Members of 21 and 23 SAS practise abseiling on 'The Tower' under the guidance of 22 SAS instructors and APTI staff attached to 22 SAS, June 1980. (Author)
102. A 23 SAS trooper kneels to fire his Sterling SMG on the COB range in Scotland. (23 SAS)
103. Two SCs of the RM SBS paddle their collapsible Klepper canoe during training. Despite the availability of DPM smocks, the SBS still use the older pattern camouflage garb as its mud brown base helps the men to blend in with the river banks and beaches where they have to lay up. (SBS)

102▲ 103▼

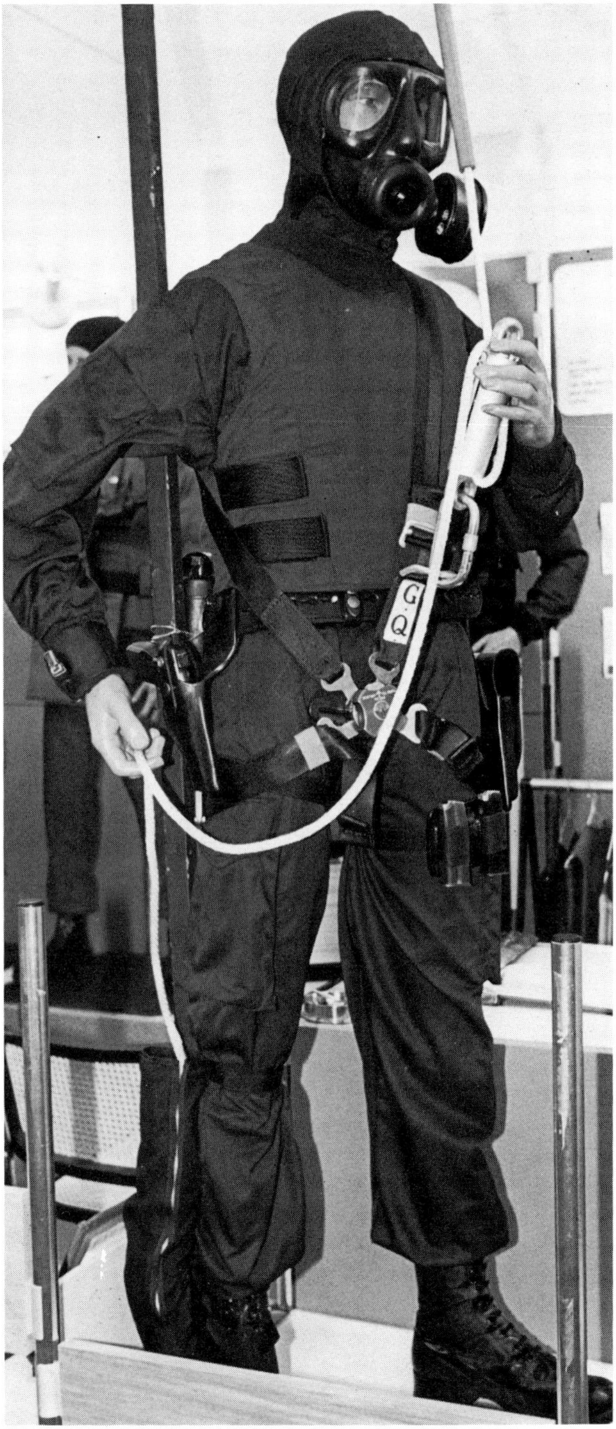

◀104 105▲

106▲

104. Cpl. 'Tug' Wilson of the Royal Marines Mountain and Arctic Warfare Cadre performs a 'death slide' from the top of Tower Bridge to the forecourt of the Tower Hotel in July 1978 to advertise the Royal Tournament (in which the Cadre, the latest RM Special Force, was participating). At that time the unit was known as the Arctic Warfare Cadre and formed part of 45 Commando RM in Arbroath. (RM)

105. This and the next ten photographs illustrate aspects of Operation 'Nimrod', the breaking of the Iranian Embassy Siege in London on 5 May 1980. Here, an example of the type of equipment available for CRW (Counter Revolutionary Warfare) troops of 22 SAS is displayed. The respirator is the standard S6, whilst the rope for abseiling is retained in a leg bag so as not to alert anybody below of the descent. At the right hip is a 9mm HP Browning with body armour cleat holster and at the left triple HK MP5 SMG pouches (magazine); at the right wrist and on the left thigh are pistol magazines.

106. The flame-retardant coverall under Bristol body armour. This equipment is almost identical to that used during 'Nimrod', although CRW gear is regularly renewed and the design altered, according to the particular squadron which is rotated through to the role.

▲107 ▼108

107. A view showing the triple pouches outside the body armour.
108. At 1907hrs. on 5 May the Metropolitan Police handed over management of the Iranian Embassy Siege to the OC 22 SAS following the murder of a hostage by the six terrorists, and at 1723hrs. the assault commenced. A group of eight SAS soldiers abseiled down the back of the building; a further six, covered by two, entered through a downstairs window; and a further four blew in a window at the front and attacked through the opening. Others – an inner cordon and a command and control group – acted in support. The photograph shows the eight SAS troopers on the embassy roof, 1920hrs.
109. 1925hrs: the eight prepare to descend in two waves.
110. 1927hrs: the first two descend. Unfortunately, the rope becomes entangled in the descender of the nearest soldier, jamming the device and causing him to break a window with his foot.

109▲ 110▼

▲111

▲112 ▼113

111. Below, the ground assault group goes in through a bottom window.
112. Behind them, a communications and support group provide back-up.
113. At the front of the embassy, another support group gives cover.
114. 1928hrs. Two of the rear assault group suffer painful burns when their clothing catches fire. They are helped by their comrades and the momentum of the rescue is not lost. The action last 11 minutes.
115. 1936hrs: five armed terrorists are dead, and one who threw his weapon away is captured and secured with flexi-cuffs.

114▲ 115▼

▲116 ▼117 118▶

116. SBS divers cache their equipment and take off their wet suits, having swum ashore from a submarine. Note that at least two of the men wear the old canvas and rubber British-pattern jungle boots still favoured by the SBS. (SBS)
117. Roped together, two SBS divers enter the water using oxygen sets. Nearest the camera is No. 2, who will observe and monitor depth; No. 1 carries the swimboard with direction setting. (SBS)
118. Royal Navy submariners bring equipment above decks to inflate and secure a Gemini craft for the flotation. For flotation, the craft is laid across the submarine's decks with the crew on board and the submarine submerges under them. (SBS)

▲119

119. The two-man Klepper canoe, seen in frame (right) and fully assembled. The Klepper was introduced in the mid-1950s and replaced both the Cockle (Folbot) and the Mk. 1**. The frame is made of Mountain Ash and Finnish Birch and the cover of Egyptian cotton treated with canoe dope. The canoe packs into a bag measuring 69 × 58 × 20cm. (SBS)

120. An SAS officer, assisted by a Belgian Para-Commando of the ESR (SAS equivalent), instructs Special Forces from Germany, Italy, Holland and Norway in US and Soviet weaponry at the International LRRP School at Weingarten in Southern Germany, April 1981. TA SAS and RM SBS Reserves attend the courses at Weingarten as part of their training. (SAS)

121. Not the monster from the deep, but a member of 22 SAS in a gillie suit used for close observation and reconnaissance. Displayed before him is the equipment he must carry into his hide, including cameras and visual aids; such were of great use to the SAS both in the Falklands and in Northern Ireland, where many recce units have been trained.

120▲ 121▼

▲122 ▼123

122. Two members of the Parachute Regiment trained in the specialist FO role. The target designator can be set on a timer, activated remotely or used in real-time to bring 'smart' ordnance down the laser reflection directly on to the target, thus doing away with the need to carry pounds of explosives.
123. SBS divers check their equipment prior to a mission off Gibraltar in March 1985. Note the wet suits and the swim-board held by one diver.
124. The four parachutes of an SBS team deploy on static line, taking the team on course for the oil tanker awaiting them below. (SBS)

124 

▲125

▲126 ▼127

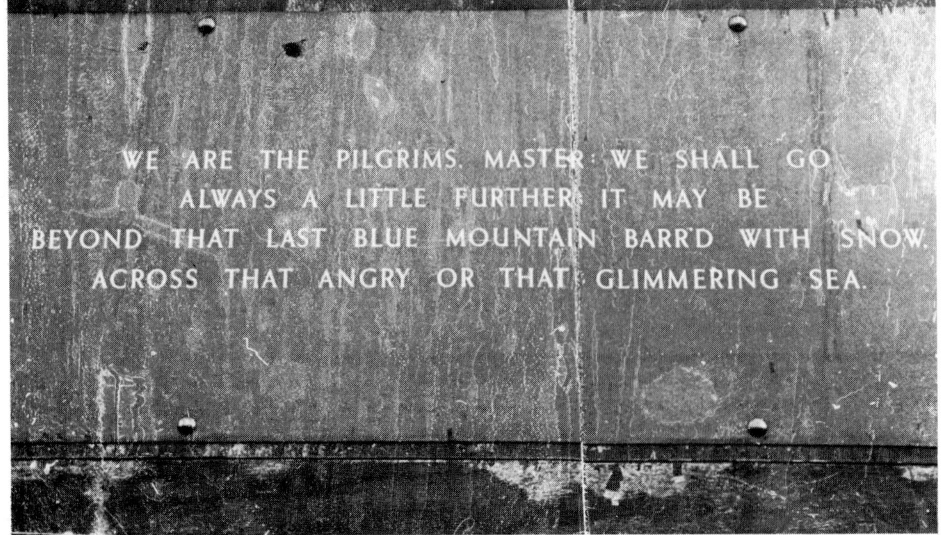

125. Pen-y-fan in the Brecon Beacons, site of the famous SAS 'Fan dance', as the gruelling 'long drag' aspect of selection is referred to. Even on the sunniest of days the cloud cover can suddenly cover 'the Fan' without warning, and a number of regular and SAS recruits and soldiers have lost their lives in this region.

126. The old Parachute Training hangar in what was Bradbury Lines, the 22 SAS Regimental headquarters since 1960. This building is indicative of the standard of accommodation and training sites available to the SAS until the new barracks was completed in 1984.

127. The inscription commemorating the SAS dead as it appeared on the famous clocktower; the other three sides of this structure carried similar metal plates which bore the names of the dead. When the new barracks, Stirling Lines, was built, the clocktower remained but the plaques were resited outside the Regimental Chapel.